10 SECONDS TO MENTAL HEALTH

200+ Tips From Nationally Known Psychotherapist/Marriage & Family Therapist Dr. Karen Ruskin

Dr. Karen Ruskin, PSYD, LMFT

ISBN-13: 978-1500964467

ISBN-10: 1500964468

Also by Dr. Karen Ruskin

Dr. Karen's Marriage Manual

9 Key Techniques For Raising Respectful Children Who Make Responsible Choices

10 SECONDS TO MENTAL HEALTH

200+ Tips From Nationally Known
Psychotherapist/Marriage & Family Therapist
Dr. Karen Ruskin

Dr. Karen Ruskin, PSYD, LMFT

INTRODUCTION

Mental health and mental wellness is the key to a happy self: personally, in terms of relationships (e.g., the marital relationship, the parent-child relationship), professionally, and in all areas of one's life. It is the seemingly small things one does or does not do, the statements one makes to one's self and others, and the choices one makes in terms of how one relates to and interacts with those in one's life, that play a significant role in one's mental health and wellness. In addition, the statements one does not state, makes the difference in one's life in terms of affecting mental health and wellness. We CAN affect our mental health and wellness! This book includes concrete do-able practical tips, real advice for real people, to help you help yourself live a life of mental health and wellness that connects with all areas of your life.

I am a strong believer that one's personal mental health and wellness is directly tied to not only the relationship one has with one's own self, but also the relationship one has with others. Thus, one will find a mix of tips in this book ranging from my advice that are statements to make to one's self, action items I recommend to do, and insights I offer as it relates directly to one's relationship with others in one's life (e.g., spouse/partner, children). In addition, I offer tips in connection to goal achievement, one's professional self, and more… My goal is to provide the reader with a helpful tip, one can say to one's self each day, that offers to touch the varied important aspects of one's life which is interconnected to one's mental health and wellness.

The past few years I have been documenting my thoughts into a mental health tip format, based upon my experience in working with couples, individuals, and families as a mental health professional. Some tips I have shared with clients, other tips I have stated while on television, other tips I have shared via social media (e.g., Twitter, Facebook). Some tips I have never shared, until now. Putting together my tips, advice I wish to share, is what this book is. It is my strong belief that personal health, relational health, marriage, dating, parenting, professional self, goal achievement- each and every aspect of one's life can be enhanced by simply taking 10 seconds out of one's day to make a statement to one's self that is positive and therapeutic. One mental health tip has the potential to be the difference that will make the difference in your life. For a mental health tip in your head can only leave your head if you choose to dismiss it. The lack of action on what one knows to be helpful can only occur if one makes that choice.

Take my mental health challenge. Read one mental health tip per day. The ricochet effect just reading one tip per day has on your life may indeed surprise you. Make the choice and be on your way to a mentally healthier self. I look forward to hearing how the tips in this book have positively affected you.

I invite you to follow me via:

Twitter: @DrKarenRuskin

Facebook: https://www.facebook.com/drkarenruskin

MENTAL HEALTH TIPS

Be mindful of whom you open your mind to. Choose to surround yourself with those who make healthy decisions. The influence just one person can have on one's thoughts and actions, is powerful.

Your kids are to be valued, respected, loved, nurtured, and cared for. Keep them out of harm's way and provide them with opportunities to grow.

As a marriage therapist for over 20 years, I have noticed that the #1 most common marital complaint is lack of attention. You can choose to do something about it. Pay attention to your spouse.

Don't wait for tragedy to strike and shake you up. Recognize what's important to you before then. Reflect on life and discover what's important to you, then nurture it.

Your child's words are just as important as how it's said (tone/body language) and what isn't said. Keep your eyes wide open to your child's words, tone, body language and overall demeanor each day.

The mind and the body are interconnected.
Make healthy choices for one and it'll affect
the other. Be kind to your mind and your body.

Consider the narrative you tell yourself about your life moments (past and current). It's those very stories that shape future outcomes and how you view yourself.

There are secrets we keep TO ourselves. It's the ones we keep FROM ourselves that, if not confronted, will lead to destruction. Confront yourself! Be honest with yourself.

Step up to the plate of life. Each day is an opportunity to get on a base or hit a home run. Don't bench yourself.

Seeking out mental health help is not a sign of weakness or failure. It's courageous to confront one's self, explore, and grow. Seek out help if your inner voice feels you desire someone to talk things through with, and/or to help you to help yourself to get unstuck.

If you haven't told someone in your life today that they are special to you and that you appreciate them, there's still time. Say it with passion! Each and every day.

Be willing to evolve, mature, enhance, and grow. Then be mindful of actively taking steps to do as such.

Do you have dreams? Take one step each day towards them. Live those passions. No one can do it for you!

If you feel controlled by your partner, and consistently put-down, re-evaluate the relationship. Healthy relationships and friendships are supportive.

How do you have a successful marital relationship? Be a partner, teammate, and lover. Be supportive, attentive, trustworthy, and kind. Make this choice today and every day.

If you stuff your feelings down or mask them, your personal emotional beaker will boil over. Open yourself up to what you have stuffed, confront those feelings and consider what steps to take to heal and move forward in a healthy and productive manner.

Treat yourself with love, kindness, and compassion.

Take ownership of what YOU can do to advance yourself professionally, enhance your relationships, and grow as a person.

Live authentically.

Some mistakes are okay. You and your loved ones can heal from those mistakes, accept them, and connect with your loved ones in response to them. Other mistakes spiral you downhill and can destroy. Make smart choices for there are mistakes that are avoidable choices if you think first with mindfulness of your actions before making them.

Be mindful of the fact that decisions you make today affect people other than yourself. Make thought-felt choices.

As you settle in each night, process your day. Consider in what areas you are proud of yourself, and in what areas you can improve.

Be mindful to make mental time to acknowledge one thing you appreciate about another in your life. Then, tell that person.

Give yourself positive feedback once per day. Giving yourself a verbal hug can go a long way for your mental health and wellness.

Feeling loved, special, and valued is the fuel that drives you far. Treat your loved ones with this in mind.

If your logical/intelligent mind is in conflict with your emotional mind, process both sides of the self. Be aware of both sides of yourself when you are making decisions. Then, take action with this awareness.

Often you can begin feeling emotionally well by simply re-framing your perspective from negative to positive. Try it!

If you know it's not right, then it's not right. Listen to your inner voice and do what IS right.

If your relationship is disconnected, take action! One person's action today can be the difference in any relationship. Don't wait for another to take action, take ownership of what YOU can do. The ricochet effect is alive and well. Your action today has the potential to lead to another person's reaction and action.

What the mind believes, the body can indeed achieve. Be the master of your own mind so that your fears, worries, and self-doubt will serve you. Don't let it control you.

Even when it seems unobtainable, take action
on your passion. It may be reachable!

Achieving your fullest potential is about drive and effort. Make the choice to achieve your fullest potential in each area of your life and thus bring your drive and effort to the table, don't leave it in the cabinet.

A few of the keys to marriage success: honesty, trust, respect, patience, and emotional/physical/sexual intimacy. So, take the key and unlock the door to a successful marriage by living these words.

Be mindfully aware of your actions and words, for it is a choice how one exists in our day to day lifestyle. Make wise choices!

There's no place for a "kids will be kids" attitude when it comes to drugs. Teach your kids from the start: "say no to drugs!"

The holiday is over (Valentine's Day, Birthday, Anniversary, Christmas, Hanukah etc.,) Now what? Do something special for your partner today! Take action every day not just on a "holiday". Be spontaneous and creative in your relationship showing the person they are super special.

All it takes is one person to choose to stop a negative pattern. Take ownership of your actions and make a healthy shift today! Choose to stop the role that you play in the negative pattern (e.g., food, exercise, your relationship communication . . . whatever your negative pattern may be).

Be mindful of the decisions you make, for it is our current choices that affect later choices and one's mental wellness.

"5 ways in 5 days to enhance your life"! Do one thing per day for 5 days. Now you got it! Keep it going! 5 days is a great goal, which leads to 6 days, 7 days, 8 days, before you know it you have went from trying to enhance your life to actually enhancing it and thus a true lifestyle change. You can do this.

Life isn't meant to be easy 24/7. When challenges come your way, know that you have the skill to confront that challenge, cope, and to solve whatever problem aspect of the challenge comes your way!

Anxieties are to be understood, confronted, and managed. They should not be ignored and they shouldn't prevent you from achieving goals. Be brave and take action!

Are you stressing out to find the perfect gift?
This is pressure you're putting on yourself.
You'll be liked without perfection, so just do
your best.

What you put in is what you get out, so make wise choices. Consider this in all aspects of your life (e.g., self, family, work...).

If you don't have a healthy personal outlet, make a decision to have one. Reading, art, music, sports, dance... What's YOURS?

Often what one needs from their mate is obvious, yet left unfulfilled. Inform your life partner of what you need, and he/she may just fulfill it!

As another week is about to begin, consider what you wished to accomplish last week. Take one step each day to work towards that goal.

Enjoy the journey you travel and make positive shifts as desired. For it is the inhalation of positive fumes that energizes the self.

Marriage and children are like plants, as are all relationships. If you water your relationships each day, they will grow. Water the blessings you have!

Some feel "blue" on Sunday evening, as it is the start of the week. Positively re-frame your mind to be glad it is the start. See it as an opportunity.

Make the time and take the time to
_____. (Fill in this blank with all
of the things one SHOULD make the time and
take the time to, such as: doing a fun activity
with one's spouse, telling your child you think
he is awesome, sharing with an employee she
is valued, take care of your body… the list is
endless. Each day make and take the time to
_____).

Balancing of work, parenting, marriage, dating, family (whichever is your circumstance) and the self, is an ongoing journey. Navigate it with the appreciation that you have things to balance in the first place. Rather than choosing to view your life through the lens of feeling overwhelmed by having these aspects in your life.

It's one thing to be disappointed in the behavior of one's children. It's another thing to put them down for it. Help educate them on strategies and alternatives. Don't degrade your children. This same concept holds true for colleagues, employees, and others in your life.

Be the door your children feel safe to walk through anytime. Let them find you with an open mind, heart, love, and patience. Be their biggest fan. This same concept holds true for how you treat your own self and your mate.

Accept that life will throw you big bumps. It's up to you to confront them, healthily cope, strategize, and take action. YOU are the driver!

Don't live with your head in the sand about your children's lives. Know what is going on and talk with them as they journey toward independence.

Take a moment this weekend to relish in the positives of your life. Be thankful for what you *do* have!

Take one step today towards enhancement
(personal, relational, work…).

SO much in life is possible when you believe in yourself. Simply be yourself and believe that this self, who you are, is capable.

Have a vision? Even if it isn't fully clear –
with drive, passion, and action your vision
will form and can be achieved by making the
choice to take one small step each day.

Have a great weekend filled with joyous interactions, personal fulfillment, and relational fun. Create this- don't just wait for it!

Be YOUR best self for you, and role model
your best you for your kids, if you have kids.
Qualities such as: work ethic, compassion,
courage, self-advocacy... Take action with
passion, love and fun.

a) Independence and Inter-dependence vs. b) Reliance/Needy,
a) Self Worth/Esteem vs. b) Negative Self-Concept,
a) Motivation vs. b) Inaction.
Choose to live the "A" life every day!

Escaping your reality with drugs and alcohol?
Consider a reality you want. Instead, use that
time and money each day to take one step
towards reality rather than escaping reality!
Choose to feel rather than numbing thyself.

Each day is an opportunity to hurt, heal, or help one's self and others. Consider your words and actions and make the choice to live a life that is rosy rather than a darkened path.

Take ownership for your behaviors and responsibility for your actions. No one else is to blame for your actions. There are always triggers that have the potential to affect one's behaviors. The moment you blame that trigger, or another person for why you are acting as you are, that is when you feel out of control of your own self which often leads to depression and/or anger. Remember: we cannot control what others do nor say nor certain life circumstances (which can be triggers). What we can control is how we respond to those very life circumstances and to the behavior of others. Thus YOU are responsible for your behavior so take ownership and responsibility for it.

If you don't like how you are behaving and feeling, consider what YOU can do to make a healthy shift.

Passion and commitment brings success in all areas of life (marriage, parenting, work, relations, health/wellness…). Bring it!

Feel like giving up? Thoughts alone don't define us. What matters is the action you take! Tomorrow brings a new opportunity- strive!

Enjoy an old passion and/or discover a new interest!

Be mindful each day of the choices you make in your relationships. Relational choices impact your personal health and wellness as well as your relationship whole.

Looking for an 'emotional pick me up'?
Every day tell yourself three things you
appreciate about: a) you, b) your life, and c) a
loved one.

The formula for success in all life areas: drive, passion, skill, hard-work, creativity, self-belief, time-management skills, and commitment. What's your formula for success? Decide what it is and live it.

What have you done this week that makes you feel good about yourself? If nothing, do something. Your relationship with yourself is such an important relationship for it is the fuel for everything in your life.

Has another day passed and you haven't taken action to enhance your relationship with your child? With your lover? With yourself? With a family member? TODAY is day one, tomorrow is day two… Commit to yourself that you will take action each day for relationship enhancement of which you will make and take a small action step.

Can a person enhance one's self personally and improve their relationships at ANY life stage? Yes! You can!

Face your challenges! When you do, there are four choices: 1) shift your thinking, 2) change "it" (whatever the challenge is), 3) discuss the situation, or 4) accept it then move on. You can choose between one of these four options or consider a combination platter. The key is: face your challenge rather than just sitting in it and stewing with no shift, no understanding, and no change. If you confront and face "it", rather than ignore it, you can then decide which choice to implement that makes the most sense to you, or which combination of the four choices is the best way to go.

Make a list of three things you like about yourself. Then, make a list on the same document of three things other people like about you. That's it! Just a little self-worth morning boost from your mind's eye and from what you believe to be the mind's eye of others.

Take action! Regarding what? Answer:
Anything! When you take action, you feel
empowered. When you feel strong, you feel
mentally well!

Self-reflection and honest analysis of who you were at different phases and stages of your life vs. who you are now has value to explore. Name one way you are different vs. the same. Is that good or bad? The qualities you adore, keep them going and bring them back into your life if they are in the past. The ugly qualities that are no more, give yourself positive feedback for making the shift. The qualities you wish did not exist in the now, make an active effort to improve upon. Remember: you cannot change what was, you certainly can change what is to be.

Knowing thyself combined with choice will help you accomplish self-awareness and self-growth to be the most fabulous you, that you can be.

Never say never, and don't stop until you've accomplished your goal! Relish in your success each step of the way and keep on achieving!

You can decide to feel up or down. The mind is powerful.

Are you proud of the person you are? If yes, why? If no, why? Take one step each day towards becoming that person you wish to be proud of. For then, you ARE that person.

Have you been putting off something on your 'to do' list? Today is the day! Do it. I'm cheering for you!

Love what IS there in your mate not what isn't there. For if we yearn for what isn't, we don't enjoy what IS.

Life includes many twists, turns, bumps, and blocks. There's no time like the now. Jump into this moving ride, grab the wheel, and take yourself to new places while experiencing your life. Truly engage in your life!

This week you'll have an opportunity to make a shift that'll enhance the course of your life (e.g., relationship, self-health, work). Take ownership of that opportunity.

Make time each day to snuggle with the person you love and relish in that moment. Escape into the joy of relational connection.

Your words, tone, body language, and actions affect your child's mental wellness, thought process, and behavior. Be wise every day with how you display these four. It is these same four that affect your own wellness. Think about it. Your words to self (positive vs. negative), how you speak to yourself in tone (do you seem like you are angry at yourself or loving and nurturing in tone), your body language and the actions you take every day – if you treat yourself with respect and of value you will feel good. Rather than treating yourself poorly. Treat yourself positively and those you love.

There can be sunshine found even in the darkest of times. Sometimes we don't recognize the sunshine within the darkness until the darkness has passed. This is a reminder that the darkness shall pass, hang strong.

List three positive things that happened today- because of you! Take ownership of how you play a part in your life journey. What are they?

Find something stimulating to do with yourself. It's our self-relationship that impacts our mental wellness and everyone around us. Have fun with you.

Strive for more in your life. Don't accept that is all there is. Yet, do relish and appreciate what you have that it is enough. Enjoy the journey of life while taking action for more. This may sound contradictory, yet recognize it is the existence of "both/and," rather than "either/or," in your choice to strive and enjoy at the same time that play an important part of self-health.

Today is another opportunity to make an emotionally healthy choice that benefits you and those you love. Upon waking- make one today!

There will be a time in your life when you are confronted by a truth that is in such contradiction to what you believed to be reality. Confront it! Don't let the shock and/or fear freeze you.

Utilize today as an opportunity to be more than who you were yesterday. What does that mean to you? Take a moment to process and consider.

Through our life journey we spot red flags.
Listen to those instinctive warning signals and
obey your inner voice of wisdom.

Consider three aspects of your life you want improved. Each day do one small thing toward each and see where you are in three months! Improved? Yes!

Create a 'Happy Timeline'. This technique helps your mind view your life through a positive lens. This technique is to create a timeline indicating each happy event you recall at different stages and phases in your life that has contributed to you being the person that you are.

Relish in the joy of possibility rather than in the pain of not knowing.

We are who we are, but don't forget you can be more than who you were yesterday. You are the only one who can make this reality happen.

If our interpretation and perspective leads to how we understand and experience an event, consider the lens of your view. Consider if the instinctive lens of which you interpret thus understand and experience past and recent events are blocks in your life. If your lens is blocking you, choose a different lens. A different lens does not mean the original lens does not have meaning to you, rather this is a choice to recognize that you can experience your day to day in altered ways depending upon the lens of which you view it. So, consider your view and decide if you feel it is accurate or if you need to wear a different pair of glasses today.

What are you thankful for? Acknowledge what you are thankful for to yourself and communicate your acknowledgment to others you care about. In this way you both experience what you are thankful for, which feels good emotionally.

Decrease and prevent chips in your relationship with clear communication of expectations. This concept applies in all aspects of life: marriage, business, parenting…

Healthy coping when affected by trauma/tragedy takes courage, strength, passion, and the will to survive/thrive. You can do it!

Are you subjective? Objective? Are you firm? Flexible? Know thyself as it opens the door to further growth.

One step may feel overwhelming, but no step (s) leads to stagnation. Take one step – it'll have a profound impact, and one step is closer to what you desire.

There are many forms of running away from your problems, but your problems will always find you! Confront your challenges and work hard to resolve them.

Your philosophical belief about child rearing matters in the development of who they are and who they become. Make wise choices for their wellness. Parenting matters.

Passion, drive, inspiration… The journey of growth never ends. It doesn't have to.

If you have a passion for something, do not give up!

People will come into your life- some for a
clip, others for longer. Whoever and whatever
the circumstances are, value the experience.

If you went through the day today and didn't tell your children that you love them, tell them right now. If asleep, then first thing tomorrow morning you should be sure to do so. Don't miss a day!

In any relationship, just feeling love for another is not enough for long term growth. You must show love with words and actions.

Make time each week to do something just for you.

All relationships encounter challenges over time. View these challenges as opportunities to find the key for relational solution-resolution.

Smell the fresh air, literally and figuratively.

Don't wait for an opportunity- make it happen!

If you want your kids to be respectful, be respectful to them and others. Want them to be responsible? Role model it.

Today is THE day to make a positive change in any area of your life. It's YOUR choice! Make one small step today, then again tomorrow…

The mind is powerful! What is a current challenge in your life? Consider how your positive thoughts can help you and how your negative thoughts hurt you.

It's easier to criticize someone else than to acknowledge your own shortcomings. Don't go the easy route. Rather, confront thyself.

Before you go to bed tonight, make it a point to share what you appreciate about your loved one. When you awake, express your care and love through words and actions.

Enjoy today, each day, the week, the weekend.
Smile with pleasure at those you care about
and those who care about you.

Loving a person vs. being in love: Consider what you feel for your partner and how that impacts the relationship. Both love types can grow with choice.

How do you express yourself? Words? Actions? At home, at work, or socially? Plan: implement a healthy balance of words and actions with interest.

Who wants to be appreciated, valued, respected, wanted, nurtured, and attended to? If you said your date, spouse, or kids- you are right! Show it! And, treat yourself with appreciation, value and respect. Attend to yourself.

Fear is a challenge to understand and confront. Then, choose to move forward toward your goal, your circumstance, your challenge that you are worried, concerned, or afraid of.

What's the 1st thing you did when you woke up today? The 2nd? 3rd? 4th? Did any include a positive statement to one's self or a loved one? If no- do so!

Create your own opportunities. When opportunity knocks on the door, confront your negative thinking, worries, concerns and dive in!

Be honest with yourself. People are skilled at fooling themselves to believe what they want. Without self-honesty, you are stuck.

Just because something is common and inferred to be normal, doesn't mean it is healthy. Choose to behave with therapeutic wisdom and be a cut above.

Consider your identity. Enhancement is
always within reach.

Wherever you are in your life journey, there is always a chance to LIVE life.

Mini moments turn into days, days into weeks, weeks into months, and months into years. Choose not to miss out! Be involved, present, and engaged in your children's world, in your world, in your partner's world.

How often do you share positive feedback about you to yourself? Do so today, tomorrow, the next day…

Tonight, share with your spouse that you appreciate who they are and that you are glad you found each other. Yes, whether you are married for three years or for 33 years.

Baby noise- DON'T ignore it or react to it in an annoyed manner. Prior to speech, communication is with noise (laugh, "whine", cries, etc.) so that you know how they feel. Respect the baby noise, be nurturing and patient for this baby learns about how to treat others, and how to view one's self, as well as who you are in their life, based upon your reaction response.

Be in touch with who your children are and who they are becoming through their life journey. What role do you play? What role can you play?

Make the time for a person you care about. Take initiative, plan and do something with that person that they'll enjoy.

Achieve your goal with these steps. First, consider your vision. Second, take action. Third, give yourself positive feedback for taking that action. Next, be patient with yourself on your journey. Then, take further action. Finally, implement steps 1-5 again and again.

The mind is very powerful! One can will oneself to feel a particular emotion after a life situation. Thus, will wisely.

Time… Cherish every moment during that very minute. For that minute in time is never to come again.

Be mindful of one's parenting. Parents truly play a significant role in who one's children are and will be.

Have you told your children today that you are proud of them? If not, there's still time left to do so. Think of a few things about their character you are proud of. Share that with them.

Imagine if most days you accessed your greatest strength and listened to your healthy inner voice. How might that impact your existence? Try it.

When something seems impossible, think: this mission is possible! The power of the mind is, well, powerful!

Instead of longing for who you could have been, use your energy for your current self. Growth is possible! Continue to work on who you are and can be, not who you could have been.

If you are feeling down, it is instinctive to make choices that further the downward spiral. Instead, choose healthy mind-body choices.

Tell yourself one positive statement about YOU! Do this today, tomorrow, and each day forward. Don't wait for someone else's positive statements, be your own best friend.

Make the time and take the time one night this week or one day this weekend to relish your time with yourself or someone special to you.

What's your dream? What do you want? What do you need? What steps are you taking? Believe in yourself.

If you feel last year was a bad year for you, name one positive thing that occurred in your life last year. Then name one positive thing so far this year.

Words plus time are a great combo platter for affecting one's mental health in terms of how one feels about one's parent-child relationship. Each day, tell each of your children something positive about him/her. This helps build their self-worth. Spend quality time with your children. The nourishment a healthy parent-child relationship has on one's mental health cannot be denied. When one's children are mentally healthy the affect that has on one's mental health as an adult is significant.

List one thing you love about yourself, appreciate about your mate, and value about your life. Do this each day. See how this affects your mood.

Communicate your thoughts in your relationship. Don't pile them in a garbage bag and think you can simply throw them out. It is the pile up of relational garbage that affects one's mental health. Verbalize your feelings in a healthy thought felt manner to allow for explorative talk.

As a new year rapidly approaches, consider what lifestyle changes you wish to make and/or a personal growth item to improve on.

If you aren't having a great day, what is one thing you can realistically do to enhance the day? Do it!

Name one complaint that people who are important to you in your life consistently state about you. Specifically consider those people of whom you value their perspective. Consider if this complaint has validity and if perhaps they are pointing out something that is accurate and if improved, your own mental health and wellness would be in a better place. If yes, would you like to consider improving?
If yes, how can you improve? Once you determine what you can do to improve, it is your choice to now take one small step each day toward improvement.

Take 30 minutes per week and label it "mental health me time". Do something during those 30 minutes that is personally healthy and relaxing.

Marriage includes: a) Acceptance, b) Tolerance, c) Appreciation/Enjoyment of what you have, and d) Doing what you can for the marriage each day. Implement A through D.

Each morning as you enter the bathroom to brush your teeth, and attend to other self care items, make it a choice to look at yourself in the mirror and state one positive thing about yourself and one thing you are proud of about yourself, out loud while looking in the mirror. Then, smile at yourself to the mirror.

It's far too easy to make statements of defeat to the self. Consider a positive statement you can tell yourself this week- say it!

The day is not over yet. There is still time to express your love for, pride in, and appreciation of others.

Do's and Don'ts of parenting: No name calling! Over time it labels/solidifies them as that. Rather, positively re-frame the negatives and implement positive parenting.

When it comes to the parent-teen relationship, validating their voice so they feel heard goes a long way in getting your voice heard by them.

No one travels through life challenge-free. It's not about whether there will be road-blocks and obstacles, but instead about how you process and deal with those challenges.

Parents say things to their spouse in front of their baby: "It doesn't matter because he/she is just a baby". Wrong! Babies see and hear! Be mindful of what you say to the parent of your baby. Babies learn sooner than many realize, the feelings a parent has in the adult-adult relationship and communication patterns and methods through observation of patterns.

If your child is being bullied, don't be afraid or embarrassed to seek out help. Children need their parents to be advocates.

Make the time and take the time to do something fun with your children this week. Bond and enjoy!

Each day is an opportunity to connect and re-connect with a loved one. Use today as that day!

Is your spouse or child behaving in a distressing way? Is your business partner? Your employee? Discuss your concerns with them. Team up together and develop a solution-resolution plan.

What have you thought today or what action have you taken today to experience your appreciation of just living? The simple fact that you can walk, talk, smell, breath, feel, touch, think, fairly healthy – are these not things to be truly thankful for? Oh yes, indeed they are. If you have not thought about this beauty and truly relished in your appreciation of what may be considered the basics of life, make the choice to value these basics fully and appreciate them.

Communication skills can be enhanced. Dialogue WITH people in your life, not AT them. This is one key technique in all your love relationships which promotes a healthy communicative relationship.

Parenting tips: be supportive, participate, be their fan, have positive feedback, be genuinely interested, care, have kindness, be patient, have compassion, and be involved.

Enjoy and relish in the simple greatness of what is, if but for a moment each day. Do this rather than only experiencing joy when there is a good outcome to something specific.

Make an active effort to try to understand a situation, or a person, of which you do not understand. For it is with understanding, even if one disagrees, that humans experience a more peaceful existence. Often the emotion of anger (which eats at one's emotional wellness) surfaces when one does not understand something or someone.

Do not try to force your belief system upon another. Rather express your belief system and recognize it is healthy for people not to always have the same opinions. Riling one's self up emotionally due to a reaction based upon a difference of opinion is a choice, just as the lens of acceptance and the positive view of differing points of view is also a choice.

Name one thing you did today to contribute positively to your mental health and wellness. If your answer is nothing, consider one small idea and do it now!

Today, make it a point to do one thing that shows someone important to you how special they are.

When home with your children during a storm, use it as an opportunity to have quality time with them. Chat, play games, and relish in parenthood! When on a car ride use it as an opportunity to have quality chat time. In essence, 'see' opportunities to connect.

Think of an event in your life that you think negatively affected you. Consider how although negative, you can also see a positive way to view it. This is the co-existence of which to see events in time. Try this the next time a negative event occurs.

Life experiences that are outside of your comfort zone play a role in your personal growth. Don't be scared to step outside of your box.

For couples: Today and every day when you wake up, consider one special thing you can do for your spouse. Each day be sure to do it!

Take 30 seconds of each day to remind yourself of one thing in life that you are thankful for.

Consider this the next time someone says something offensive to you: what another person says, says more about them then it does about you.

Think about how you would describe yourself in three words. Think about what three words you would like to use to describe yourself. Take action to be that person so the words you would like to describe yourself as, will be a reality. You can grow!

Every day, relish the gift of motherhood, fatherhood, parenthood. Relish individualism. Relish your singlehood. In essence, whatever is your life, whether it be as a single person, as a married person, as a parent, as a boss, as an employee, take a moment to relish and treasure it. Relish, relish, relish…

What are three life skills you want your children to possess? What have you done to ensure that your children have acquired these? What can/will you do? Do you have that life skill? If you do not, make it a choice to work on that life skill.

Consider this: Drive beyond failure, turn right, turn left, keep going, in order to eventually succeed thereby reaching a desirable destination.

Every day gives us the opportunity to interact with others. Think before you act, for it makes a difference in the short-run and the long-run.

What makes you feel a healthy, warm feeling through your mind and body? Actively implement THAT special something today!

Marriage is a growing journey: never with decisions of finality, but rather forever rediscovering.

Take a theatrical slow-motion-deep-breathe in, then a total slow-motion-exhale. Next, smile with your teeth exposed. How do you feel?

Strive to reach the moon AND relish in the "mini-s" of your life that are right in front of you.

It's your daily interactive choices with your loved ones that affect you, others, your relationship now, and your relationship in the future. So interact lovingly.

Food affects mood. Be mindful of your food choices.

Exercise affects the chemicals in one's brain thereby affecting one's mood. If you are not including physical activity in your life, make the effort to include it.

You are a capable human being, choose to be capable not incapable.

How you dress presents yourself in how others view you. How do you wish to be seen? Consider this in your clothing choices in the varied contexts of your life (e.g., job interview).

Take a photo every now and again, and print it out the old fashioned way by putting it in a picture frame. Hang up the picture on your wall so you can see it each day. Memories are nourishing to the emotional spirit.

We all experience some type of tragedy, a trauma, as we navigate the journey of life. Choose to live life and fight on! I did and do and so can you! Bring the you that you can be, and thus are, every day.

Smell, taste, see, and touch the mini moments and the basics of your life. Embrace it all.

Tell yourself you are a winner.

We all have self doubt and insecurities that emerge at different moments throughout life. It is a choice for those thoughts to drive one's car. Visualize clouds clearing your self doubt and insecurities away. Then, visualize the emergence of your self confidence. It is with this clarity of sight that you will drive far.

ACKNOWLEDGEMENTS

Thank you to my dear husband Seth and my precious son Jeremy for your love and support of me and all my ventures.

Thank you Anne Fritzson. A lovely college student, my 1st intern. Your enthusiasm, energy, and diligence helped this book come to fruition. Such a sweetheart, perhaps someday I will consider having an intern again.

Thank you to Mark from Angel Editing for smoothly transitioning my written document to a book.

Thank you Ken Berman for your photography skills and speed of completion adapting to my schedule.

Thank you to my friend Lisa Shooman for reading my final version at crunch time.

Thank you to my colleagues at Dr. Karen Ruskin & Associates, for being a part of my life. Every day I am reminded how blessed I am to have a hard working clinical team of whom helps so many with their skill and care of and for the clientele who come through our doors.

Thank you to my clients for 20+ years of whom have trusted in me to share their life challenges with me. I value the opportunity to continue to provide real solutions for real life problems.

Thank you to my parents Neil and Vivian Bailes. I am confident your love and interest during my childhood played a significant role in the person I became in adulthood, which in turn filled me with passion for helping others to help themselves get to a better place.

Thank you to my friend Geri Picow. What am I thanking you for? For being a true friend for 40 something years. And, 40+ more.

Thank you to the FOX News Boston Morning and Evening Team. You have provided me with the platform to share my insights with regularity during my 'Ask Dr. Karen' segment, as well as your trusted go-to expert addressing timely topics from the Psychotherapeutic lens. I value the art of providing education on air in an effort to touch the masses. In addition, I thank the national FOX News Channel, FOX Business Network, and all of the producers, anchors and various networks (e.g., ABC, Discovery, Lifetime, MTV...) of whom have opened their doors to me so that I may provide practical tips, offer real solutions for real life problems, and provide cutting edge insight. It is a privilege to play a part in the de-stigmatization of the therapy profession and the very concept of mental health and wellness.

35411223R00126

Made in the USA
Charleston, SC
09 November 2014